Systemic Questioning Techniques

for Specialists and Executives, Consultants and Coaches

The importance of questions in the profession

by Hans Patzer

Table of Contents

1. Introduction

In professional life, problems usually arise again and again, which are then sometimes discussed endlessly in the team. It doesn't matter whether the discussion is conducted in a meeting room, via video chat or via e-mail. During a meeting, it can happen very quickly that everything keeps going in circles and there is no solution in sight. An efficient way of working, therefore, also requires the right and meaningful conduct of conversations. A lot can be achieved, especially with the right question technique. For this, however, the participants must first know various question techniques and should also move outside the classic closed or open questions.

Systemic questions are therefore of great importance in every position, especially in professional life. It is also important to recognize that "whoever asks leads". You should therefore use systemic questioning techniques so that you can also take on the role of leading the conversation. In this book you will learn what the meaning of systemic questions is and which different types exist. Practical examples will help you to recognize the meaning and the application even better and to implement them afterwards. Because the right question technique needs to be learned just like taking over the conversation.

Systemic questions offer a good opportunity to get more information or to achieve a change of perspective. This makes it possible to successfully break through a discussion that moves in circles. Question techniques are therefore used during job interviews, when solving problems in a company or with customers, or in conflicts within a team. The correct use has to be learned so that you can achieve the desired effect and really reach the ideal solution or obtain further information. Have fun immersing yourself in the world of systemic questions and the possibilities they offer!

2. The importance of systemic questions

Systemic questions are a special **form of questioning technique**. Since there are different types of questions, the term "systemic questions" is a generic term. Systemic questions are particularly well known and frequently used not only in professional life but also in coaching and therapy. The most important result of using these questions is that completely **new perspectives emerge** and are perceived. Without these specific questioning techniques, it would be much more difficult and protracted to achieve the same results. This becomes obvious very quickly when the questions are used in practice.

The importance of the question techniques is therefore enormous for all those who work in the professional field with customers, clients or employees. It always makes sense to look at existing **problems** from a **different point** of view and not always stubbornly from the same perspective. The questioning techniques are therefore particularly important for people who work with other people and have to solve problems. Basically, certain question techniques can be assigned for the right communication. In addition, systemic issues are of great importance in any form of **conflict resolution** and **problem solving**. This applies to both the professional and the private sector. Finally, in order to develop one's own personality and lead a happier life, certain harmful behavior patterns must also be recognized and changed.

Systemic questions regarding a basic assumption are not suitable for being used as a self-help technique. Therefore, **at least two persons** are always required for the application in order for a change to be achieved. Systemic questions are also of great importance in group discussions. In a one-on-one discussion, just as in a group, new views can be gained and other solutions found. At the next meeting at work you can already check in which direction the conversations go and when or how solutions are found.

Surely you have encountered systemic questions more than once—perhaps only without recognizing them directly in the first moment.

In addition, it is also helpful if systemic questions are recognized as such in a conversation. Exactly in this way awareness arises of which direction the questioner would like to steer the conversation. Perhaps you also know the feeling of being manipulated or pushed in a certain direction. With knowledge of the systemic questions you will recognize in each case if such an influence is made on the discussion process.

3. The use of systemic questions

Of course, such systemic questions can also be used without further ado in private life. This certainly allows one or another problem to be viewed in a completely different way. Or it can be solved. Perhaps a different perspective will help, for example, to resolve the current dispute with your partner or the tense situation with your friends. This shows that systemic questions can be used well in many areas. However, these questions or the techniques behind them are particularly popular in the workplace because in working life problems that initially appear unsolvable often arise, long meetings in which people chew on a problem again and again without ever finding a solution. These are the exact situations in which systemic questions really represent a good option.

Some situations where systemic questions are used:

- There are problems with a current project and the project seems to be doomed to failure

- Customer XYZ causes problems and cooperation could fail

- Profit has declined and needs to be increased again

- Sales figures decrease or costs in the company have risen sharply

- There are interpersonal problems that affect work

- The acquisition of new customers does not work as hoped for

- The competition within the industry has increased strongly and the existence of the enterprise is threatened

- Colleagues are bullied in their departments

- Numerous layoffs endanger smooth operations

- During an interview, as much information as possible about the candidate should be obtained

This not exactly short list could now be continued at will. The examples already clearly show the possibilities of the new form of questioning. It is therefore very interesting for many areas of professional life to deal with these techniques because without suitable communication and without a view of other options it is everything but simple to gain enough information and find the beginnings of a solution. Finally, humans simply tend to turn rather in circles and, crucially, not necessarily change their own perspective. This **changed approach** is also very important in professional life for more success and faster processes.

The problem is first and foremost that you have to adjust to a new technique of asking questions. It is very easy to fall back into old patterns during a conversation or discussion. This means above all that you have to practice the new questions and techniques intensively. Therefore, it can take a moment until the individual options can really be implemented in all discussions. A good possibility is therefore to start slowly and use individual question types. For example, start with circular or solution-oriented questions. These are question types that are even easier to use. The same applies to the scaling questions, which can always be used without problems. This also provides a good introduction to the further discussion, as you will learn in the next chapters.

To start directly with wonder questions or with paradoxical questions could be overstraining—both for yourself and your interlocutors! In addition, it should also be noted that it is not appropriate in every conversation or in every situation to take over the conduct of the conversation. For good reason there are seminars in many larger enterprises, which invite all high-level personnel to practice discussion guidance. In seminars on discussion guidance or the better communication systemic questions and their employment are always amongst the various topics. An exact representation of the individual question types with examples for better clarification can be found in the next chapters.

In any case, it makes sense to deal with the topic on a private level at first then gradually train in the individual question types. Especially at the beginning it is interesting to use systemic questions in your private environment. In this way, insights can be gained and you will surely find out how you can also achieve changes in your professional life. For the self-employed, **learning systemic questions** is also of great importance as it can significantly improve your **dealings with customers, employees and business partners**.

4. Advantages of the changed question

Who doesn't know that in professional life, a topic can sometimes be discussed in meetings for hours on end and always be reassessed? But a solution is not so easy to find and quite often the employees behave like lemmings who stubbornly follow a well-known order. Such meetings strain the nerves, increase working time and do not really lead to a result in the end. So it makes sense to approach problems differently. It is precisely this different approach and **change of perspective** that makes sense behind the systemic issues.

But why should you really concern yourself with systemic questions? What is the point of dealing with the different types of questions and perhaps changing one's own form of communication in the long term? At this point you will learn more about the many advantages of the changed question. When looking at the advantages, a change in one's own communication certainly makes sense and is directly viewed less critically.

The advantages of systemic questions in an overview:

- ✓ Fixed behavior patterns can be broken and changed

- ✓ New and creative solutions are emerging

- ✓ The conversation turns much less in circles

- ✓ Existing resources are recognized and used

- ✓ Problems are viewed from different angles

- ✓ The questioner receives a lot of information from their counterpart

- ✓ It's possible to make problems look smaller and less scary

- ✓ The dynamics in groups and teams are recognized

- ✓ Offers good possibilities for the subsequent solution of the problems

✓ Offers a good introduction to the conversation

The very extensive advantages show here the many possibilities that systemic questions offer to you. In many cases, a classical, unstructured conversation does not bring any new insights at all. So it makes more sense to approach this problem differently. You will surprise your counterpart and certainly make him think. Therefore, it is always useful to include the different types of questions in your own repertoire and to practice professional conversation intensively. In the following pages you will learn about the different variants of systemic questions. There are certainly many more than you might think at first.

5. The different variants of systemic questions

At first, it certainly sounds as if systemic questions are several options all grouped under one main category. This is not the case because there are already some **question variants**. Knowing these is the first step for the later application in practice, which then really leads to a goal, because systemic questions differ fundamentally from classical questions. With the classical options, the most common questions are open questions, which invite one to tell a story, and closed questions. In the case of closed questions, the interviewee only answers yes or no, since the question was formulated accordingly. Systemic questions, on the other hand, consist of several other components and can be divided into these categories:

5.1 Circular questions

A common problem is always looking at a situation from the same perspective. Circular questions are about **changing this perspective** and looking at the current situation from a different perspective. This is how **new ideas and approaches** are created that can really lead to success. Such an approach is particularly interesting if the person with the particular perspective is present during the conversation because then the point of view can be changed so that given feedback is likewise effective. As a rule, we don't know or hardly know how we affect others. Only then does it become understandable why certain points of view are perhaps very personal and not very goal-oriented.

Understanding circular questions is easier in any case if there are some examples. The following questions belong to circular questions and thus also to systemic questions:

- How would the customer feel if you met him with this attitude?

- Put yourself in the shoes of your colleague. How would your colleague react in this situation?

- Why does your counterpart react in this way to your behavior?

- Imagine talking to your friends or partner about it. How exactly would they react and what advice would they have on the matter?

- What does your boss expect from you and from what perspective does your boss see this situation?

- Try to imagine an external observer. How would this uninvolved observer react in the situation?

What exactly are the advantages of circular questions?

The special thing about these questions is that they enable a change of perspective. Through this change much more can be achieved than you might think right now.

The advantages in a nutshell:

- ✓ You learn to put yourself in other people's shoes

- ✓ A new point of view of the other person is presented

- ✓ Breaking open old and stuck thinking patterns

- ✓ Obtaining information about the interviewee

- ✓ Helps the questioner to recognize certain perspectives and to recognize the dynamics in groups or among colleagues

5.2 Solution-oriented questions

Negative thinking and the exclusive concentration on a problem very often prevail in discussions. **The bigger the problem**, the more the **focus is placed on it** and the more negative the overall perspective. Here, too, the point of view and the starting point have to be changed. Solution-oriented questions that focus on possible solutions are a good option. The advantage of this approach is that the problem is not so much put in the foreground. The overall discussion becomes more positive and it is much more likely that solutions will actually be found. It is precisely this that is prevented by a negative view that is purely focused on the problem.

Some examples of questions that are solution-oriented:

- Are there any possibilities that should currently be used?

- How has such a problem been solved in the past?

- Which procedure works best?

- When did it go particularly well and what was done differently at this point?

- What difficult situations have been solved by the department?

- Which factors are particularly important for success?

The view of the positive certainly does not only work with one's own thoughts. It always makes sense not to remain too much in negative thought patterns and not to give nourishment to the hopelessness that so easily arises. This type of question is therefore a good option if solutions for the current problem are to be found in a really timely manner.

The advantages in a nutshell:

- ✓ The view is strongly directed towards positive things

- ✓ Existing resources and opportunities are more easily recognized

- ✓ The awareness that solutions are possible and available is strengthened

- ✓ The view is directed towards helpful colleagues or people in the surrounding area

- ✓ Leads to a solution faster than the eternal discussion about the existing problem

- ✓ Negative thoughts are not in the foreground here

5.3 Hypothetical questions

"What if I did?" Hypothetical questions are a good option to change one's perspective in professional life because very often new insights arise that would otherwise not have been considered at all. Maybe you won't get the solution to a problem directly, but thinking around the corner and experimenting with thoughts are important things—this way you can **increase the creativity of the respondents.** Some example questions in this case would be:

- What would you do if time didn't matter now?

- What would your solution look like if you had a budget without limits?

- What would you do if you were no longer afraid of failure or had to be afraid of failure?

- What would your dream job look like and what do you do in this dream job?

It's actually the popular **"what if?" game**. The most interesting thing is which answers and possibilities come out of it. After all, **creative solutions and approaches** in professional life are often of great importance. But to activate these resources, it is important that respondents look beyond their own horizons. But beware: no one should be condemned for their answers. Making fun of the answers is certainly also wrong. Because the goal of hypothetical questions is it important to welcome seemingly completely crazy answers that perhaps are nevertheless helpful.

The advantages in short form:

- ✓ Stimulate creativity

- ✓ Ideas come up that would not be considered otherwise at all

- ✓ The answers can provide a valuable basis for further action and ideas about the possibilities

5.4 Reasoning questions

Very often in our profession we only do what we are asked to do and our own actions are hardly ever properly questioned. This is of course different in higher positions, but even then many things are often done without questioning them. The reason for these questions is therefore the consideration that the results can also change if the **motives are questioned more closely**. Questioning the motives of others is certainly always an interesting possibility. Some example questions would be here:

- Why are you so convinced of that?

- How did you come to this conclusion?

- Which experiences are the basis of your current opinion?

- How sure are you exactly that the problem can be solved in this way?

- Can you give me a more detailed description of your approach?

Just as with solution-oriented questions, reasoning questions are also about **questioning one's own views**. Putting oneself in other people's shoes and explaining why one proceeds in exactly the same way or why one considers this way of working to be the only true one can change a lot. This is exactly the meaning behind reasoning questions, which are very popular, especially in professional life. In addition, these particular questions are also very often used in therapy as seldom do people consider their actions thoroughly or reflect upon them.

The advantages in a nutshell:

- ✓ A deadlocked behavior is questioned

- ✓ The search for reasons for certain ways of working is the first step towards a change

- ✓ The questioner gets a better insight into the respondent

- ✓ Helps with understanding the people in the team or in the group

- ✓ Very one-dimensional views are recognized and can be broken open

5.5 Wonder questions or hypothetical questions in the extreme form

Actually, wonder questions also belong to the previously mentioned **hypothetical questions**. But they are so **extreme and unlikely** that they still get their own category. In any case, this type of question among the systemic questions helps you to think differently and perhaps come up with completely new ideas in this way. Some examples for such wonder questions, which certainly bring interesting results:

- Imagine winning the lottery tomorrow. What happens next?

- Tomorrow you suddenly have an offer for a seemingly unattainable dream job in your mailbox. What changes in your life?

- The current problem is suddenly solved in the next hour. What happens afterwards?

- What would your current work look like in a perfect world without problems?

You should definitely practice and master miracle questions; because the procedure is rather unusual interesting answers can come out. It is not a must, but the people questioned may surprise you with very **interesting answers**. However, it is important with these questions that such a form of the discussion guidance is **announced**, especially when wonder questions are asked in this way for the first time. With the appropriate announcement, however, surely interesting and new answers can be found.

The advantages in a nutshell:

- ✓ Ensure that respondents gain new motivation and think positively

- ✓ Focus on solving the questions

- ✓ Very creative answers are possible

- ✓ Imaginative ideas can be the starting point for a real solution

- ✓ Directs the gaze away from the current problem and the negative point of view

5.6 Scaling questions

A popular variant and a good opportunity for assessment are scaling questions, which are therefore frequently asked. Actually, this type of question is very simple, since you only have to ask, "On a **scale of 1 to 10**, where do you rate the problem?" This can be implemented in very different situations and this type of question is particularly suitable for correctly assessing a problem. In addition, the **complexity is reduced** and the problem is directly less frightening than before. After all, there are very often problems that appear to be particularly complex and virtually impossible to overcome. Scaling questions are then a good starting point in these moments. Here are some good examples of such questions:

- How do you rate the current problem on a scale of 1 to 10?

- Compared to a previous problem from the same area: Where do you rank the current problem on a scale?

- On a scale from 1 to 10: How satisfied are you with your work right now?

- How high do you estimate your current stress level on a scale between 1 and 10?

Giving a problem or a current state an assignment or a kind of note can be very helpful. Above all, this representation on a scale makes clear the extent of the current problem. Perhaps the problem is smaller in comparison than initially assumed. The clear division always helps to **reduce fears** and to perceive a problem as much **less overwhelming**. In addition, it is certainly the type of question of systemic questions that is the easiest of all to learn. After all, it does not take so much to formulate such a question in a way that fits the situation. Respondents can also easily answer the questions and, unlike many other types of questions, they are much less off-key.

The advantages in a nutshell:

- ✓ A more precise form of self-observation is stimulated

- ✓ Very good introduction to a topic and an opportunity for further processing

- ✓ The questioner gains many insights from the answer

- ✓ The question is put in a very simple form

- ✓ Applicable in any situation without problems

- ✓ Changes and differences in workflows are recognized more quickly

- ✓ Progress is also recognized

- ✓ The fear of a problem is reduced

5.7 Paradoxical questions

Here a little creativity in the head is necessary. For paradoxical questions are not at first about really solving a question or finding a good solution. Rather, the question is completely **reversed** and turned upside down. This can lead to some very crazy and definitely very creative ideas. It does not even have to be about ideas that can be implemented immediately, but such solutions can emerge from these thoughts. It's about thinking in a different way or about possibilities that don't fit into any drawer. However, a little time is needed in any case in order for such questions to be really implemented.

Some examples of paradoxical questions in professional life:

- What do you have to do to make sure the project fails?

- How do you manage not to get your promotion on any account?

- How do you safely get rid of potential customers?

- What can be done to make the current problem worse?

- Which measures help you to become really unhappy?

Just as with the miracle questions, a small **advance warning** is also useful with the paradoxical questions, otherwise the interviewees will quickly feel overwhelmed or irritated. After all, a completely different approach than usual is necessary to answer the question correctly. It's sometimes very **helpful** to see what doesn't **work at all**. Because right at this moment a situation can be turned around well.

If something very bad is achieved through a certain behavior, perhaps the exact opposite will help to solve the problem or at least to get a good deal closer to this solution. Therefore you should also include paradoxical questions in your repertoire. But you will definitely have to practice them as they are a little harder to implement than some of the other question types. Sometimes no other question techniques help and this kind of question helps to find a solution after all. After all, it can never hurt to tackle current problems anew.

The advantages in a nutshell:

- ✓ A problem is strongly exaggerated and thus put in the right light

- ✓ Turns a situation around

- ✓ Shows what is not possible and sometimes leads to the exact solution of the problem.

- ✓ Amazes the interviewees and makes them think

- ✓ Helpful in stuck situations

- ✓ Creates space for new, creative solutions

6. Systemic questions: what knowledge is required?

Systemic questions are therefore a specific form of questioning. But this also means that this question is not suitable in every situation and for everyone in professional life. The basic prerequisite is the **knowledge of the appropriate questions** and the sensitivity to exactly what can be achieved with these questions. In all communication, it is ultimately important to **respond to the** other **persons** and to communicate accordingly. You can therefore only achieve something with systemic questions if you fully involve and listen to your counterpart. A certain amount of knowledge about communication itself, about conducting conversations and about the effect on a psychological level is therefore very important.

In addition, you should gradually acquire the knowledge or rather the feeling when each type of question really makes sense. Are rather **quick results in a short time** particularly important? Then **solution-oriented questions** are suitable. If above all **creative** and completely new approaches and ideas are needed, then **hypothetical questions or wonder questions are** better used. If, on the other hand, stuck work processes and ideas are a possible problem, you should try solving it with questions of justification or circular questions. In a short time, however, little or nothing can be achieved with miracle questions or paradoxical questions. You should not forget this when applying the questions in practice.

In the following chapter you will learn by means of practical examples how you can put systemic questions into practice but also what effect the individual questions can have. It is precisely this effect that can be observed again and again when the individual question techniques are put into practice. Often the results are astonishing and in this way you learn much more than with simple open and closed questions. Then the information obtained in this way only has to be used in practice.

Procedure for successful implementation of the systemic questions

The knowledge and possibilities of the special question technique are now known—only the exact procedure for the correct formulation and insertion of the questions is still missing at this point. After the practical examples you will also find some hints that will help you with the formulation and the right approach. It is precisely the practical implementation that definitely poses the greatest challenge when it comes to systemic issues. At this point you will find some ideas on how you can better approach the formulation and ideal handling of the situation. You should always start with the problem that is causing the conversation.

The following procedure is recommended for systemic questions:

1. In the first step, clarify the exact problem and the reasons why you should speak. Some questions will help you and make sure that you can narrow down the topic:

- What's the problem?

- What is the impact of this problem?

- Why exactly is this thing problematic?

- Who is involved and who can be addressed?

- Who can't you talk to?

- Are there people who have no interest at all in solving this problem?

- Are there aspects that are obvious to all the people involved in the conversation?

2. Then you should concentrate on putting the current problem in a context with other problems and perhaps filter out existing differences. This also helps to narrow it down and to find out how to proceed now. Ask yourself or narrow down the following things:

   - Who is affected?

   - What is the context of the problem?

- When did the problem first appear?

- Since when and in what context has the problem arisen?

- Are there conditions and moments when the problem does not occur?

- Does the problem change or does it always remain the same?

3. Use W questions to narrow down the problem. For the solution and the best formulation of the questions, it is very important that the existing problem is narrowed down as much as possible. W questions and of course all aspects around the context and the persons concerned will help.

4. Use systemic questions. You should not formulate the questions exactly but rather make **keywords** and write them down. This requires a little more practice in the beginning but becomes a habit after a while. At this point you can decide which question types you will use to achieve the most in this case.

It is important to know that systemic questions alone can hardly solve a problem. Rather, it is a different and interesting form of questioning, which is often ignored otherwise. In addition, it is about the **acquisition of information** and **entry into a conversation**. Ideas and suggestions often emerge, which then need to be examined more closely in due course. Some examples can be found directly in the next chapter and in these examples you can see that it is a part of the conversation and not the whole content. The information gained still needs to be processed and implemented in a meaningful way. However, this method is very well suited for changing perspectives and gaining information.

Perhaps you are wondering at this point whether there are things that should be avoided urgently for successful use of systemic questions. A conversation can, of course, be excellent and contribute to gaining information but it can also amount to the exact opposite and go completely wrong. There are some things you should avoid directly to at least reduce the likelihood of failure.

Less helpful techniques and procedures

It is definitely possible to cause anger or irritation with systemic questions because of the nature of the questions. Therefore, you should always select and ask the questions carefully so that you really only get the answers you want and no annoyed reaction. You should therefore better avoid the following things:

- Ask several questions at once and thus overburden the respondent or the group

- Ask questions with a threatening undertone that are reminiscent of an interrogation

- Ask questions that are very unclear or diffuse, leading to confusion

- Pretend to give the answer or literally put it in the interviewee's mouth

- Ask numerous questions in quick succession so that there is no possibility of answering them at all

- Asking leading or suggestive questions (An example: Any question that begins with "Is it not so that...")

It can also make a lot of sense to give the respondents the opportunity to adjust to the completely new and unusual technique before using systemic questions. This way you can also avoid irritations from the beginning and make sure that the respondents adapt to new techniques. Perhaps you will also explain briefly what it is about and that it is mainly about gaining information and a different perspective. No interviewee is to be put on the spot and there is also not simply a right or wrong answer. It simply takes a new approach to achieving results and gaining new insights.

7. Practical examples

You certainly have a better idea of the meaning and possibilities that systemic questions offer you. However, as a rule, the knowledge is not yet quite sufficient to enable implementation in practice in a procedural situation. This implementation becomes simpler as does the idea of the possibilities in the event that you can see the situations more clearly. Here you will find a number of practical examples explaining why these questions make sense in this situation.

Have fun reading and good luck trying it out! Because the systemic questions are ultimately not only suitable for managers but also for all other employees who are in professional discussions this often enables better and faster solutions to be found. One thing you should always keep in mind when using the systemic questions: The person asking the question conducts the conversation. If this is not desired or not possible, you should consider carefully whether you can and should apply the questions in this situation. The following examples are all short extracts from conversations and show how and why systemic questions could be used well.

7.1 Practical examples of problems with customers

Sooner or later, there will be problems with customers in almost every company. This can happen on many levels and it is not uncommon for such difficulties to jeopardize the success of a company. In the worst case, dismissals or insolvency can result. Therefore, we start our practical examples here with some situations in which systemic questions can be used to solve customer problems.

7.1.1 Situation A: A customer has not paid his invoice and delivers a lot of turnover

In the company, this is a customer who has unfortunately already become conspicuous and who does not want to pay the last invoice despite reminders. The turnover is not good without it and it is to be feared that with a judicial dunning procedure the customer will give up cooperating. In return, the company would be able to protect itself against default, which would place a heavy burden on the reserves. Ms. Meyer, the head of the accounting department, therefore briefly sits down with her team and the marketing staff.

Ms. Meyer: "Let's assume we look into our accounts in the next hour and the customer has paid. What would happen then and how would we proceed?"

Team member: "Of course, we are happy that we don't have any non-payment for the time being. But the question is whether we will continue to work with the customer. Or will there only be an advance payment in the future?"

Ms. Meyer: "We would probably save a lot of effort with an advance payment. The question is then whether the customer would get involved or go to other companies. But of course we can't work with a customer who never pays or only pays extremely late..."

Here a **miracle question was** inserted. This is the **opposite of a paradoxical question**, which you will learn more about in the next example. Miracle questions are among hypothetical questions and strongly exaggerate them. As in this case, it is a matter of finding an immediate solution to the problem. It can certainly help to face such problems with very crazy ideas and then actually solve them. However, this is not a procedure that can be implemented very quickly—you should therefore have a little patience when answering the questions.

7.1.2 Situation B: Major customer Mayer complains about recent quality

The online marketing agency has several medium-sized and small customers in addition to its major customer Mayer. Nevertheless, much really depends on the major customer due to the very high turnover. The question at this point is how the customer can be satisfied again—and whether there really are losses in quality or other difficulties with the customer. The head of customer service, Angela, has therefore brought all employees together for a discussion.

Angela: "Suppose Mayer, our major customer, terminated our contract tomorrow without notice and made us feel bad about other customers. What would we do?"

Team member: "From now on, we would have massive losses in sales and would have to make more efforts to get the other customers not to react to the negative news accordingly. The timely search for new customers would be an option."

Angela: "Do you think we can keep the key account or would it be better to switch to new customers?"

Team: "The major customer seems to have problems with cooperation from now on. There is no visible change in the quality, although it is always difficult to measure, especially with the articles. If we're looking for new customers now, we can avoid the worst-case scenario."

In this case you will see how to deal with a **negative increase of the facts** and what possibilities arise then. It is a **paradoxical question that** exaggerates everything and helps to put the problem in perspective or to deal with it at all—because it often turns out that the current problem is perhaps not so huge or unsolvable. Then a little distance helps to solve the whole thing. Paradoxical questions also have the potential to show how or why the problem is maintained.

7.1.3 Situation C: Many returns burden a small online shop

Online shops are still booming, at least when they offer good products. But returns in particular can be an enormous burden and pose a serious threat to small businesses. This is exactly what is happening with the small shop Flying Bags, which has concentrated on very special leather bags in unique designs. The many returns of the last orders ensure that the total turnover is actually rather small. Now, in a meeting, the employees are looking for possible strategies that can help to ensure that the customers actually remain customers.

Jan asks the other members of the team: "Which approach works best?"

Steffie: "I have heard from other companies that customer loyalty is not strong enough when returns occur."

Jan: "What measures did the other companies take to strengthen customer loyalty exactly?"

Steffie: "There is partly the offer that three or five euros will be credited to the customer's account If no return is made. Or e-mails are written to customers, asking them about their experiences. Small gifts in a parcel can also boost customer confidence and reduce the number of returns."

Jan: "Thank you very much for the good solutions. I think we should test several things. Let's start with the e-mails. In addition I find that a credit note at a value of three euros is meaningful when a return is not taking place. This not only encourages customers to keep the order but also encourages them to order again."

Solution-oriented questions are a very good option for such problems in order to receive **interesting suggestions as quickly as possible**. In addition, this approach takes the focus away from the existing problem and towards a more positive view. In most cases and in case of difficulties like in the existing case, meaningful ideas are also mentioned. It is therefore a matter of activating the existing resources and not concentrating exclusively on the problem.

7.1.4 Checklist for questions regarding customer problems

Solving problems with customers as quickly, efficiently and thoughtfully as possible is simply one of the tasks in a company. However, this is not always so easy because many employees concentrate on the problem and not on a solution.

You should consider these points when formulating questions in these situations:

- ➢ Have there been similar problems in the past?

- ➢ Are the resources to solve the problem already available?

- ➢ Can small things already help or do very big steps have to be taken to solve the problem?

- ➢ Is the company at stake or could other customers be found relatively quickly?

- ➢ Does it make sense to contact people from other teams?

- ➢ Are the problems due to the wrong work or approach or are they really due to a loss of quality or service?

7.2 Practical examples of increased competition

Increased competition, collapsing sales or the shift from stationary retail to online business: these situations unfortunately occur very frequently. Companies that do not act in a timely and intelligent manner will soon be faced with serious problems as a result of fast-moving developments. Below you will find three practical examples and see how systemic questions can help in dialogue and perhaps also in brainstorming.

7.2.1 Situation A: A traditional company is threatened by new competition

For many years, the idea was unique in German-speaking countries: the traditional company Inka Bags limited itself to accessories and dresses imported from the Andes region. Customers were able to create their own patterns, colors and materials. At first everything was handled in a retail shop and for about eight years now there has also been an online shop, which also works well. In the course of globalization and increasing opportunities, however, there is now a strong and exclusively online competitor that also undercuts prices. The ten employees in Germany are now meeting in a crisis meeting.

Managing director to his team: "On a scale of 1 to 10, how high do you estimate the threat from the new provider?"

Staff member Anna: "I would estimate the threat to be a six."

Staff member Jan: "I would estimate the threat at a seven."

Managing Director: "Why do you rate the threat so highly on the scale?"

Employee Anna: "The offer is interesting and very similar to ours. However, I have seen some reviews that say the quality is not always optimal. The seams of the pockets are not quite stable and some scarves seem to have stained when washed."

Employee Jan: "They are cheaper than us and offer an extensive assortment. But they don't have a shop and the online shop can't be compared to ours in the ranking."

In this case, the very **simple technique of scaling questions was** used. Of course, this approach would also work without the justification and would then simply be there to assess the threat more realistically. In this way, employees lose their fear and free their minds for other solutions and approaches.

Here, however, it is also advisable to ask for reasons for the assessment. This interview offers a very good starting position for further suggestions and solutions. Perhaps the company concentrates on the elaboration of very high quality as a unique selling point. Or the focus can be placed on further optimizing the ranking of the online shop—by highlighting the many years of experience and the local partners. However, the conversation certainly does not rotate in a negative way and it is possible to find good solutions that will really help.

7.2.2 Situation B: Turnover in a retail shop has collapsed due to online competition

The small boutique in downtown Düsseldorf has built up a loyal customer base over the years. What is special about the shop are the exclusive dresses and shirts from Italy as well as the handmade shoes. Good advice and a noble ambience have always helped to attract somewhat wealthier customers. In 2018, sales fell sharply as fewer and fewer customers shopped in the store. Now the owner, Mrs. Müller, is talking to her employees in order to find an urgently needed solution.

> Ms. Müller on the group: "Assuming that the budget and the time would play no role at all now. What possibility could we use then?"

> Employee X: "If time and budget are unlimited, we could set up a very special online shop. One that offers more than just pure products with pictures and in different sizes. We could offer a personal online consultation and install software in which customers could see how the garments fit by uploading their pictures."

Employee Y: "We could build a website like this and then introduce a certain designer every month. Then we could present complete outfits in our special style. Above all, we have to show our customers what sets us apart from other providers. When money and time don't matter, we should be unique."

This dialogue is a brief introduction to a possible approach in which ideas are collected. This is a **hypothetical question, which is one of the** systemic questions in this case. In this way, the owner Mrs. Müller can collect ideas on how to save the business. Of course, in the real world money and time do play a role. However, lessons can already be drawn from previous proposals. The thought of an online shop in this situation was certainly obvious. But what are special are the special elements of the shop, which aren't quite as self-evident and easy to find out.

7.2.3 Situation C: A blog generates less revenue through many similar blogs

About five years ago, Corinna started her blog about travel. She concentrated particularly on the aspect of backpacking as a woman. The focus is on travelling alone and safely and many exotic destinations are presented in more detail. A good additional income was the result of the blog, so Corinna has had a business partner, Tobias, for three years now. However, advertising revenues have dropped dramatically in the last six months and there are now a number of similar websites from other women. That's why Corinna and Tobias have arranged to have a video chat.

> Corinna: "Assuming you talk to your girlfriend about the current problem. How would she see it and what would she expect from a website like ours?"

> Tobias: "Hmm, well, I'll try to put myself in her place. So pictures are always very important to her, she has already said and shown this several times. She probably wouldn't find the pictures on the website to be the best yet."

Here Corinna used a **circular question**. Tobias should put himself in another person's shoes and try to find out what the other person thinks or how he sees the problem. Here many answers can be the consequence and it's not always the answer that must help in the end with the search for a solution. But it always makes sense to **look at** the world or rather the particular problem from a different **point of view**.

The next step now could be, for example, that the images of the page are really more closely viewed and optimized. Or maybe it should be a better appearance in the social networks after all. But if you put yourself in the shoes of other people like partners, friends or even customers, this can really be very effective when looking for a solution.

7.2.4 Checklist: This is what you should keep in mind in similar situations

In these special situations, it is important first of all to deal precisely with the situation and the problem.

When formulating the systemic questions, pay attention to the following points:

- What is the current problem and is it possible to find a solution in this round?

- Does it make more sense to talk with the whole team or with individuals?

- Which information can best be obtained?

- What is the current mood in the team like and how optimistic are the employees when it comes to solving the problems?

- Which employees (in a larger team) are the best contacts for this problem? Does it perhaps make sense to interview employees from completely different departments and thus obtain new ideas?

7.3 Questions to be asked during an interview

An interview is a classic basic situation for the use of systemic questions because with the questions you can get a lot of information out of the interviewees. You can find out much more information than with any other questioning technique—often respondents are not even aware that they reveal so much. This may sound like manipulation at first, but it is a common way of gathering information and finding out whether a candidate is suitable for the job in question.

7.3.1 Situation A: Max applies for a position from a different position

Max studied marketing and has some professional experience in online marketing. However, he is now very interested in a position in content marketing and would like to develop more in the direction of online editor. The professional experience is therefore not yet really available and so in this case the personnel department wishes to learn more about Max and his motives.

Human Resources: "In a perfect world: What would a working day look like for you and what things does it contain?"

Max: "In a perfect world, my day would consist of exciting tasks so that it never gets boring. Above all, writing would take up a very large part of my day because I can really get into it. Nice colleagues and a pleasant working atmosphere would round off the day."

The questions with **"in a perfect world"** belong to the **wonder questions**. These are popular **information-gathering** measures as respondents may be surprised. In this case, Max has now revealed rather few surprises, but this is partly due to the rather tense situation in the interview. However, the personnel department learns that varied tasks, a good working atmosphere and a lot of paperwork are important for Max. In the further course of the interview it would then become clear whether he is a suitable candidate for this work or not. Here, too, systemic questions form only part of the conversation and do not constitute the entire conversation.

7.3.2 Situation B: Human Resources Department wants to receive information from Tanja

Tanja has applied for a position in the company's marketing department. She has professional experience and makes a really good impression on the personnel department. Some questions are intended to better test her problem-solving skills as these things are of great importance to the job.

> Human Resources Department: "Suppose your client is very dissatisfied with your work and threatens to withdraw the order. Put yourself in the shoes of the customer once and then consider how the customer sees this situation."

> Tanja: "Once I assume that the customer is dissatisfied because of some details and the communication, I would like a clarifying conversation from his point of view. Best with suggestions on how to solve the details better. Many

customers already feel calmer when they are taken more seriously with their worries and then properly responded to."

In this case, the HR department uses a **hypothesis** and associates it with a **circular question**. The **problem** mentioned **is fictitious** and currently not really present. This is actually always or almost always the case in job interviews. It is simply a question of looking at the person's perspective and how he or she would solve the problem. In this case Tanja shows that she responds to her customers and that communication is very important. These are certainly important characteristics in the context of marketing activities and cooperation with customers.

7.3.3 Checklist: Important considerations before using systemic questions in the interview

Especially in an interview, systemic questions offer a multitude of possibilities to get more information than in classical interviews. Before formulating the questions, however, you should consider some aspects so that you really get the information you want. In contrast to the following examples, the aim here is not to solve existing problems. Rather, it is about fictitious situations or about putting the acquisition of information in the foreground.

So watch out for the following:

> What position is the candidate applying for and what tasks are there?

> Is there a lot of customer contact or do tricky problems have to be solved?

> Does the applicant already have work experience?

> Which information is available and which things are still very important for the job?

> Are there areas or properties that could possibly become problematic?

7.4 Systemic issues in conflicts within the team

When working in a team or when several people work together, conflicts can arise very quickly. The respective personalities, motivation, work and many other aspects play an important role. If such conflicts are not properly addressed, this may not only affect interpersonal relations but clearly also the work itself. Systemic questions offer new approaches and many possibilities to change something and to develop different perspectives to solve the problems.

7.4.1 Situation A: Employee Max has recently made many mistakes to the annoyance of colleagues

Actually Max has always worked quite well and dedicated himself to his work. This did not lead to any major problems with his colleagues. But in the last two months the mistakes have accumulated and it does not seem that much has changed in the private or professional situation. That's why the head of the personnel department is now talking to Max about it.

> HR Manager: "Max, I was told that there have been some problems with errors from your side lately. What do you think your boss, Christina, expects from you in this situation?"

> Max: "I think that Christina would expect the work to be delivered flawlessly. But lately I've had problems with my colleagues. This also led to a lack of concentration and made my work harder than usual."

> HR manager: "If you had to put yourself in the shoes of your colleagues, how would you see yourself in the situation?"

> Max: "I think I would also be annoyed and would first of all try to talk to my colleagues. Maybe I could help and that would iron out the existing bugs and maybe there would be fewer bugs in the future."

Justification questions are practical and helpful at the same time as circular questions in such situations. The first thing is to find out exactly why someone behaves in this way in a certain situation. If we have problems here with colleagues and the non existent but expected help, then this should not be neglected.

It doesn't sound as simple as that because the right questioning technique is required for this information to be revealed at all. The interesting thing is that in such a case the interviewees often do not even know in advance why they really react in this way. Recognizing worn patterns of behavior is therefore also very often the goal of systemic questions. This procedure is particularly suitable and recommendable for this information acquisition.

7.4.2 Situation B: Trainee Anna was made a victim of mobbing by a colleague

The intern has been employed in the company's marketing department for two months. A few days ago, Anna turned to the personnel manager because her colleague was mobbing her and she could no longer stand this situation. The personnel manager has therefore first of all asked the above-mentioned colleague for an individual interview in order to clarify this unpleasant situation as well as possible.

> Personnel Manager: "I asked you here to talk to you about the allegations of mobbing against our trainee Anna. I would now like to ask you to put yourself in Anna's place as far as possible. How would you react if Anna behaved this way towards you?"

> My colleague: "If Anna had behaved towards me in this way and said these things, I would probably feel a little offended, however not really hurt since such a remark could not make me that way. After all, it was a criticism of her work and not of her person."

The personnel manager: "So in your opinion it was a criticism and not a remark that should be seen as bullying? Then I would suggest at this point that we get Anna to understand this and try to find a sensible solution."

Depending on the exact situation, it is certainly particularly difficult to find a solution and have a good conversation within conflicts. In this case, the personnel manager used the **method of circular questions.** Also possible here would have been **questions of justification**. Basically, it makes a lot of sense in such conflicts that people put themselves in other people's shoes. In the case of a dispute, mobbing or other attacks this is certainly the case, since often only a change of perspective leads to a result.

7.4.3 Situation C: New colleague Tom is excluded from the team

Tom has just joined the accounting team, which has been in existence for around five years. There are currently two colleagues and another colleague employed there, who also do something in their spare time from time to time. However, Tom doesn't find the right connection here and feels marginalized and unhappy because he has been with the company for three months. That's why department head Nina is now looking for a discussion with the entire team to find out more about the cause.

Nina addressing the team: "Tom has been with you for a good three months now. Nevertheless, the cohesion and team spirit of the past is no longer so noticeable. Jana, what would your partner think, for example, about why is it so difficult in the team at the moment?"

Jana from the team: "Well, my partner is always looking for the similarities between people. He would consider whether Tom might have similarities with the rest of us on which to build."

Nina: "Are there any similarities that could perhaps strengthen togetherness?"

Tom: "I think we all like sushi. Maybe we could try a dinner together at the Japanese restaurant in the city center?"

Team + Nina: "Yes, we are very happy to do that."

In the end, everyone agrees that they want to have dinner next Friday. In any case, it is a chance for better integration or for it to exist at all.

In such a case, **circular questions** sometimes reveal the **causes of the problem.** Sometimes, however, this is not helpful and it can happen that individual conversations are still to be sought. Or maybe the new team member is simply a person who is not compatible with the other colleagues. But it always makes sense to first look into the reasons and see where the problem could be. In this example, eating together can break the ice, but it does not have to succeed. This must therefore also be taken into account when using such question techniques.

7.4.4 Checklist: This is what you should keep in mind when dealing with systemic issues in conflicts

In conflicts particularly, the wrong technique can destroy or aggravate a lot. That is not to be ignored completely and therefore you should always consider before such a discussion exactly which questions are meaningful and appropriate.

You should pay attention to the following points:

- ✓ Who are the persons involved in the conflict?

- ✓ Is a group discussion possible or are individual discussions the better solution?

- ✓ Do the people have an appropriate relationship with you so that they will even tell you helpful things?

- ✓ What exactly is the conflict?

- ✓ Were there similar conflicts in the past and, if so, how were they resolved?

8. Conclusion

Systemic questions thus offer many opportunities to take on a different perspective and solve problems. Apparently hopeless situations can be loosened up and it is also possible to minimize the fear of a problem or a situation. The breaking open of established behavior patterns and the observation from the point of view of another person also support changes. However, the questions and the practical examples also show that this is not a method to be learned at very short notice. For long-term changes, better conversations and faster problem solving, It is important to practice the new types of questions intensively.

Meaningful conversation requires empathy and the ability not only to listen but also to respond to the respondents. Therefore, quite a lot of skill is required for the perfect use of systemic questions. With time, the exercise means that you can take over the conversation and arrive at meaningful solutions more quickly. Even very complicated and procedural structures or problems can be solved in this way or approached differently. Systemic questions are therefore certainly an aid in communication, which should be known above all in professional life. These questions are particularly well suited for starting a conversation or taking on other perspectives.

Hans Patzer

Legal notice and imprint

This work, including all contents, is protected by copyright. Reprinting or reproduction, in whole or in part, as well as storage, processing, reproduction and distribution with the aid of electronic systems, in whole or in part, is prohibited without the written permission of the author. All translation rights reserved.

The contents of this book have been researched from recognized sources and checked with great care. Nevertheless, the author does not assume any liability for the topicality, correctness and completeness of the information provided.

Liability claims against the author, which refer to damages of health or material kind, which were caused by use or misuse of the presented information and/or by the use of incorrect and incomplete information, are in principle impossible if on the part of the author, as can be proven, deliberate or accidental negligence are not present. This book is no substitute for medical or professional advice and care.